Want More?

Experience greater
spiritual intimacy and
power through the
Holy Spirit baptism

Tim Enloe

EM Publications
Wichita, Kansas

Published by:
EM Publications
P.O. Box 780900
Wichita, KS 67278-0900
www.enloeministries.org

Printed in the United States of
America.

International Standard Book Number:
0-9749739-0-4

Library of Congress Catalog Card
Number Pending.

Acknowledgments

The greatest acknowledgment belongs to the Holy Spirit. Thank you for revealing Christ to me and helping me reveal Him to others.

This book would never have been written without the consistent encouragement of my wife. Rochelle, you are my best friend, and I thank God every day for you!

Without our godly parents' influence, Rochelle and I would never have known the person and power of the Holy Spirit. Thank you.

Special thanks to Nancy Lambert. Your editorial expertise is truly a gift from God.

Thanks also to Dr. Gordon Anderson for your valuable insight and suggestions.

Dedication

   I dedicate this simple book to our
three sons: Braedon, Dolan, and Barret.
May you grow to be mighty men of God,
full of faith and full of the Holy Spirit!

Want More?

Contents

Introduction
  9

1 Five Encounters with the Holy Spirit
  14

2 What Is the Baptism in the Holy
   Spirit?
   28

3 Who Can Receive?
  41

4 How Can I Be Sure That I Have
   Received?
   47

5 How Do I Receive?
  60

6 Receive Now!
  76

Want More?

7   What in the World Just Happened to Me?
     85

8   How Can I Stay Full of the Holy Spirit and His Power?
     88

9   How Can I Let the Power Out?
     99

10   For Those Who are Struggling to Receive
     105

About the Author
     109

Want More?

Introduction

I Wanted More!

I was desperately hungry for
more—more of God's presence, more of
God's power, more of God. Many of my
friends had experienced a special encounter with the Holy Spirit that had dramati-
cally changed their lives. I wanted to
experience it also, I wanted more!

For years I had heard about the
Holy Spirit and how He desired to
empower believers, but I was never able to
break through and personally receive His
touch. I was always close, but evidently
never close enough. I felt like such a
failure.

This August evening was looking
no different. The after-church time of
prayer was winding down. I had worn
out yet another crew of people who were
trying to "pray me through". I felt
frustrated and discouraged as they
dispersed.

Now finally alone, I tried to ignore

the feelings of failure as I knelt in the front corner of the building and set my heart again to worshipping Jesus. It wasn't long, though, before I began to sense God's presence in a new way. My eyes filled with tears as He seemed very close. Suddenly and gently, the Holy Spirit came upon me. I struggled for a moment in total surprise—grateful, but not sure what I should do next. I continued to kneel down but felt unusually weakened by His presence.

On one level, I was trying to understand what was happening. On another, I felt like I needed to say something but was not exactly sure what to say. Then I took a big risk. Words of English were not expressing what was in my heart. Frustrated with myself and my inabilities, I decided to simply trust God to help me communicate.

That's when it happened! I opened my mouth and began speaking, but this time, words that were strange to me—but words I knew were from God—came out. As I spoke, I felt the Holy Spirit literally flowing through me!

Just like the early Christians in the Book of Acts, I had encountered Jesus as the Baptizer in the Holy Spirit.

That experience opened the doorway to the "more" that I wanted so desperately. In fact, the baptism in the Holy Spirit has made a great difference in every area of my Christian life; that's why

Want More?

I love sharing about it with others.

We'll talk more about my experience later on, but let's talk about you right now.

Relax!

Since we come from different backgrounds, each of us has different ideas that give unique perspectives on the Holy Spirit and His ministry. Some may view the work of the Holy Spirit with great excitement and anticipation while others may have great concern or reservation. Some are expectant while others are just plain scared to death.

Be confident; the Holy Spirit and His work are not mystical or strange. People are the ones who tend to get spooky about the Holy Spirit. In fact, the Spirit gets blamed for many things that He has nothing to do with!

The Bible tells us that Jesus is the One who baptizes in the Holy Spirit. John the Baptist said of Jesus,

> I baptize you in water, but he [Jesus] will baptize you in the Holy Spirit (Mark 1:8).

If you are fearful, relax. Our heavenly Father gives every good and perfect gift (see James 1:17), so God has something good for you!

If you are feeling unsure, examine

Want More?

the Scriptures with me in the following pages. Our journey together is upon solid, scriptural ground.

If you can identify with my early frustrations, be encouraged. You can receive this beautiful gift from God today.

I can't wait for you to understand and experience my friend, the Holy Spirit, in powerful new ways!

Want More?

For Reflection...

1. Have you ever been frustrated and disappointed when you struggled to receive something from God?

2. Have you ever felt dissatisfied with your relationship with God, like there was something more that you were missing?

3. What would your ideal relationship with God be like?

Want More?

1

Five Encounters with the Holy Spirit

Jesus spoke extensively about the Holy Spirit during the hours before His arrest and trial (see John 14–16). He unfolded a wealth of understanding about who the Spirit is and what He desires to accomplish in our lives. Christ let the disciples know that the Holy Spirit would come and take over His role of "helper" and "counselor".

> But I tell you the truth: it is for your good that I am going away. Unless I go away, the Counselor will not come to you; but if I go, I will send him to you (John 16:7).

All through the Scriptures we can see glimpses of the Holy Spirit moving.

14

Want More?

He is revealed in ever-increasing detail as the story unfolds. By the time you get to the end of the Book, you find that His work and ministry are absolutely essential in our lives.

The Scriptures reveal five distinct ways we can continuously encounter the Holy Spirit throughout our lives. Each one is very different, having a special purpose and result. Each interaction reveals God's desire to build a true, intimate, and lasting relationship with us. Each one is not just an event but a beautiful ongoing process that allows us to enjoy and grow in our relationship with God.

Convicting

The first encounter that we can have with the Holy Spirit is called conviction.

> When he [the Holy Spirit] comes, he will convict the world of guilt in regard to sin and righteousness and judgment (John 16:8).

Romans chapter one tells us that every person should be able to recognize a grand Designer behind the universe. We should be able to see God's creative order and artisanship in nature.

Want More?

> The wrath of God is being
> revealed from heaven against
> all the godlessness and
> wickedness of men who
> suppress the truth by their
> wickedness, since what may
> be known about God is plain
> to them (Romans 1:18–19).

We can observe beautiful flowers
and babbling brooks; we can hear the
birds chirping and feel the warmth of the
sun's energy. But instead of submitting to
the Creator-God, we choose to think that
all of this beauty came from a chance
explosion of primordial slime! We would
rather believe in the fairy tale of evolu-
tion than come to grips with our personal
sin problem.

The first chapter of Romans reveals
the problem; we try to cover the truth of
God with our wickedness in order to
avoid accountability to a holy God.
That's how deep our sinful nature goes.

We need to encounter the Holy
Spirit so He may

> convict the world of guilt
> in regard to sin and
> righteousness and judgment
> (John 16:8).

Without His help we cannot see
our need for God! Since God is not
willing for anyone to perish in hell, He

Want More?

sends the Holy Spirit to reveal our guilt of sinning against Him and to convict us of God's reality.

This is how much God loves us! Out of love then, God sends His Spirit to show us just how much we need Him. The decision is then up to us; will we accept this divine revelation in humility or continue to ignore His pleading?

Conviction is not necessarily a one-time occurrence, but, in fact, it should be an on-going process. When we first choose to accept the Spirit's conviction of sin, we ask to be forgiven for sinning against God. That moment we are born again—in right relationship with God—and have begun the process of Christian maturity. But we will still need the Holy Spirit to call us to greater personal purity by convicting us of any areas of unrighteousness. Our holiness should then increase as we grow in Christ.

If it has been a long time since you have sensed His conviction, be cautious that you have not chosen to ignore the Spirit pleading with you to grow in holiness.

Another important dimension of His convicting work is that it inspires us with the hope that we can actually change! He wants to help us become more like Jesus.

We need to encounter the Holy Spirit as "Convictor" on a regular basis.

Want More?

Regenerating

The second encounter that we have with the Holy Spirit is called "regeneration" or "renewal". Titus explains the Spirit's role in the miracle of salvation:

> But when the kindness and love of God our Savior appeared, he saved us, not because of righteous things we had done, but because of his mercy. He saved us through the washing of rebirth and renewal [regeneration] by the Holy Spirit (Titus 3:4–5).

The Spirit is the one who miraculously renovates us into a new creation. First Corinthians 5:17 confirms this:

> If anyone is in Christ, he is a new creation; the old has gone, the new has come!

Being born again is the greatest miracle anyone can ever experience. Following that miracle, you can make it to heaven in a sick body; you can enter God's kingdom with fractured emotions, but you cannot enter heaven unless you have been born again. Jesus Himself said,

Want More?

"I tell you the truth, no one can see the kingdom of God unless he is born again" (John 3:3).

Examine your life for a moment. Will you enter heaven? Many think that living a good life will enable them to escape hell. They say, "I'm basically a good person. Sure, I've made mistakes— I'm only human—but I've never killed anyone. I was baptized as a child. I give to the United Way. God sees all of this and knows how hard I try."
But we have created a god that conforms to our image by assuming we know what God thinks is acceptable. The biggest error we can make is choosing our own standards for entering heaven. We select standards that are attainable for us solely through our own efforts, working to gain God's acceptance. Yet the Bible shows us otherwise:

> For it is by grace you have been saved, through faith— and this is not from yourselves, it is the gift of God— not by works, so that no one can boast (Ephesians 2:8–9).

God doesn't allow each of us to invent a standard to enter heaven; He has already chosen the standard. We must let go of our subjective ideas and cling to the truth that we must be born again by accepting His forgiveness.

If you have not yet been born again, why not ask Christ now? God has made it so easy. He is not looking for you to complete some great task; all He wants is for you to acknowledge that you have sinned against Him and accept that Jesus died for your sins. Ask for His forgiveness right now. It's that simple!

You will experience God's forgiveness and the Holy Spirit's regeneration the moment you ask.

> If we confess our sins, he is faithful and just and will forgive us our sins and purify us from all unrighteousness (1 John 1:9).

Once we are born again, we assume the joyful, daily responsibility of living for Christ.

Indwelling

The third encounter we have with the Holy Spirit initiates a truly precious and intimate relationship through His indwelling presence and ministry in our lives. "Indwelling" means that He moves in the moment we are born again!

The Apostle Paul told the Corinthian Christians,

Want More?

> Don't you know that you
> yourselves are God's temple
> and that God's Spirit lives in
> you? (1 Corinthians 3:16).

He told the Roman believers,

> And if anyone does not have
> the Spirit of Christ, he does
> not belong to Christ
> (Romans 8:9).

All those who have been born
again have the Holy Spirit living and
abiding inside them. You don't "get" the
Holy Spirit at a later time; you "get" Him
from the beginning of your new life in
Christ! You cannot receive the Father
and Son without also receiving the Holy
Spirit, for God is one (see Deuteronomy
6:4).

Many well-meaning believers who
are baptized in the Holy Spirit misunder-
stand this important point. They ask
another believer, "Do you 'have' the Holy
Spirit?" They are really asking the person
if he has received the baptism in the Holy
Spirit. Every believer has the Holy Spirit
living in them, but the Bible plainly
shows that the Spirit baptism is different
from and occurs after this indwelling
experience. We will discuss this in more
detail shortly.

The Bible promises that all of the
benefits of the Spirit's ministry are yours

Want More?

when you are born again—simply because you now "have" the Spirit dwelling in you. Jesus promised that His indwelling Spirit would help (or comfort) us, teach us, remind us of Christ's words, lead us into all truth, speak to us, show us what is yet to come, glorify Christ, and reveal the things of Christ to us (see John 14:16–17; 16:13–15).

Thank God that He sends His Spirit to dwell in people like us!

Maturing

The next encounter we can have with the Holy Spirit is through His maturing work. This is the life-long process where the fruit of the Spirit grows in our lives as we mature spiritually.

> But the fruit of the Spirit is love, joy, peace, patience, kindness, goodness, faithful-ness, gentleness and self-control (Galatians 5:22–23).

Christians should naturally bear fruit, the Spirit's fruit, and these nine characteristics define the very character of Christ. My favorite verse in the Bible is where Jesus said,

> All that belongs to the Father is mine. That is why I said the Holy Spirit will take from

Want More?

what is mine and make it
known to you (John 16:15).

The Holy Spirit will reveal the
character of Christ in your life as you
daily yield to His ministry.

I hope you have experienced this
maturing work in your life; my life is
significantly different because of the Holy
Spirit's work in me. For example, my
reactions are different. I used to be a
"panicker," but now I find my life is
increasingly ruled by His peace. I used to
consider myself patient (as long as I didn't
have to wait very long), but now I
frequently respond with a patience that
certainly doesn't come from me.

Another dimension of the maturing work of the Spirit in our lives is
holiness. This is closely related to His
convicting work as He continuously
reveals areas that need to be changed in
us. Never forget His first name—Holy!

God's safety net around our lives—
our conscience—can become more and
more sensitized to pleasing Him. My own
experience demonstrates this very well. I
used to be able to watch most television
programs and movies—even if they were
laced with violence, bad language and the
lot. There have been many occasions that
the Holy Spirit has whispered His
displeasure in my ear, and I have obeyed
His instruction to change the channel
because a conscience seared by wrong

Want More?

input can have devastating implications in a believer's life.

The Holy Spirit will help you to grow in holiness as you mature in your walk with God; just make sure you're listening to Him!

Empowering

The final type of encounter a person can experience with the Holy Spirit is His empowering or anointing. This is when a person is energized with the Spirit's power to minister (share his or her faith, pray for miracles, etc.). Both the baptism in the Holy Spirit and the nine manifestation gifts of the Spirit (see 1 Corinthians 12:8-11) fall under this category.

We see isolated cases of people being Spirit empowered in the Old Testament. The Spirit came upon the prophets, some judges, and several kings. However, Jesus fulfilled the old covenant by His death and resurrection. This opened the veil for everyone who believes to enter the Holy of Holies and experience all that God has for His children. Peter identified the Spirit baptism as the very thing Joel prophesied:

> This is what was spoken by the prophet Joel: "In the last days, God says, I will pour out my Spirit on all people"

24

Want More?

(Acts 2:16–17a).

Thank God that we live under the New Covenant!

The book of Acts is our practical handbook concerning the Holy Spirit empowering people. From its second chapter we find God freely giving His power for people to use in His service. We find Apostles and non-Apostles healing the sick, casting out demons, speaking in unlearned languages and performing the miraculous. Ordinary and undeserving people who were touched by God stepped into the place of God's overwhelming strength and wisdom.

Ordinary people just like us!

The gateway to this power is found first in Acts, chapter two, on the Day of Pentecost. The believers gathered to receive this empowering, the Spirit baptism, as they obeyed Christ's command:

> I am going to send you what
> my Father has promised; but
> stay in the city until you have
> been clothed with power
> from on high (Luke 24:49).

So then, God desires each one of us to continuously encounter the Holy Spirit through His convicting, regenerating, indwelling, maturing and empowering

Want More?

works.

The Holy Spirit's ministry to us is rich and diverse but it always focuses on magnifying Jesus in us. No wonder Christ said,

> The Holy Spirit will take from what is mine and make it known to you (John 16:15).

Let's now follow our pathway to the final encounter of the empowering work: the baptism in the Holy Spirit.

Want More?

For Reflection:

1. Have you thought much about the importance of the Holy Spirit's continuous ministry in your life?

2. Can you honestly say that you are born again? If not, please consider asking God to forgive your sins right now. God's Holy Spirit will move into your life and give you a fresh start. Tell someone else what has happened in your life today (see Romans 10:9-10).

3. Think of some occasions when the Spirit has convicted you of sin or has challenged your conscience.

2

What Is the Baptism in the Holy Spirit?

The baptism in the Holy Spirit is the primary empowering from God that New Testament believers can experience. Jesus promised it before and after He was raised from the dead (see Luke 24:49, Mark 16:17, Acts 1:8). It was so important that He gave this order to the first Christians,

> "Do not leave Jerusalem, but wait for the gift my Father promised, which you heard me speak about. For John baptized with water, but in a few days you will be baptized with the Holy Spirit" (Acts 1:4–5).

According to Scripture, New Testament believers should follow the

Want More?

Lord's command and be baptized in the Holy Spirit.

Not the Same as Salvation

The Spirit baptism is a first step in your development after becoming a Christian. The book of Acts shows us that new believers were expected to experience the Spirit baptism shortly after they were born again. In fact, the Early Church held baptism in water and baptism in the Holy Spirit as essential primary steps in a new believer's discipleship.

Most people who feel that they do not need the Spirit baptism do not fully understand it. They may not recognize the overwhelming benefits that the Bible promises will flow from the Spirit baptism into their lives.

The baptism in the Holy Spirit (empowering work) is not the same thing as being born again (regenerating work). Remember, all you need to be adopted into God's family is to be born again. The baptism doesn't make you any more or less a child of God. The Spirit baptism is all about greater spiritual intimacy and power!

Luke, the author of Acts, went out of his way to show us that everyone who received the Spirit baptism was clearly already born again. Acts records that it was the next natural step that believers took after they were born again.

While ministering at a church in Mississippi some time ago, I met a man who had questions along these lines. He told me his story after the service. He was a minister in a denomination that did not believe in the baptism in the Spirit. In fact, he had always been taught that the Spirit's regenerating work and empowering work were the same thing. He had joined the Air Force and was on his way to begin service in the Orient when he made this fateful trip to the Mississippi church. This Air Force minister just happened to attend the Sunday we were sharing on the baptism in the Holy Spirit. I was preaching on a topic he didn't believe in!

He was silently arguing his trained point of view with many of the statements I made. When I mentioned that the Bible shows everyone who received the Spirit baptism was already born again, his mental debate stopped. He quickly scanned the book of Acts and discovered it was true! There was a difference between being born again and being baptized in the Holy Spirit. He had an unclaimed promise to receive.

This man had been trained to reject and refute the baptism in the Holy Spirit as wrong teaching; however, he was convinced otherwise by his own Bible! He was one of the first of many to receive this beautiful gift that evening. I later received an e-mail from him in which he told me how powerful and life changing this experience was for him.

Want More?

What are the areas that you are most dissatisfied with in your walk with God? In what areas do you long for "more"? Can't they be summarized this way: not enough intimacy with God and not enough spiritual power in my life? The Scriptures reveal how the baptism in the Holy Spirit directly answers these great needs, providing two distinct benefits to all who receive.

Internal Blessing: Greater Spiritual Intimacy with God

The first benefit of the baptism in the Holy Spirit is something that is personal, just for you. He desires to immerse you in His Holy Spirit—to saturate you! Haven't you been hungry for spiritual refreshing? Haven't you longed for greater intimacy with God?

This immersion is indicated in Acts 1:5 where Jesus said,

> John baptized you in water,
> but soon you will be baptized
> in the Holy Spirit.

He was comparing something the

Want More?

disciples had previously experienced with
something new He wanted them to
experience now. Jesus paralleled John's
water baptism with a baptism or immersion in the Holy Spirit—something that
Christ Himself would perform, as John
the Baptist had prophesied:

> I baptize you with water for
> repentance. But after me will
> come one who is more
> powerful than I...He will
> baptize you with the Holy
> Spirit... (Matthew 3:11).

The Greek word for "baptize" is a
word that literally means to be immersed
or covered over. It does not mean
"slightly dampened" or even "high
humidity"; it means totally submerged.
Let's back up for a moment. Who is
the Holy Spirit? Remember that God is
one Being, yet He is revealed in three
eternally distinct Persons: Father, Son and
Holy Spirit. (I think you are already
figuring where I'm going with this). His
stated desire to baptize you with the Holy
Spirit means that God wants to IM-
MERSE you in HIMSELF! Our Creator
wants to have a personal, intimate, lasting
encounter with you!
When Jesus told His disciples that
they would be immersed in the Holy
Spirit, His declaration also had significant
meaning for them culturally. The

Want More?

disciples were living in a time of priestly ministry. The Jewish priests were the only ones who could minister the sacrifices for sins—and they did this on distant platforms as special mediators between man and God. Furthermore, it was the high priest who ministered the blood of sacrifice before the Ark of the Covenant—and that only once a year. At that time he would splatter the symbolic blood of atonement on the lid of the Ark, between two golden cherubim's wings formed on either side of the lid.

The disciples may have often wondered what the inside of the Holy of Holies was like, but they would never know firsthand because by Jewish law they could not go in and stand before the Ark.

However, Jesus told His disciples, a group of non-priests, that their new covenant standing would enable them not only to catch a glimpse of the Ark but also to be immersed between the wings of the Cherubim!

We too can be immersed between the wings of the cherubim—in the fullness of God—because the baptism in the Holy Spirit is an immersion in God Himself. This immersion is first for our personal benefit. It is a spiritual experience that refreshes and blesses us internally, giving us an intimate encounter with God.

This is precisely what happened on the Day of Pentecost. Acts chapter two records the details:

> Suddenly a sound like the
> blowing of a violent wind
> came from heaven and filled
> the whole house where they
> were sitting. They saw what
> seemed to be tongues of fire
> that separated and came to
> rest on each of them. All of
> them were filled with the Holy
> Spirit and began to speak in
> other tongues as the Spirit
> enabled them (2:2-4).

This intimate immersion affected both their spiritual awareness and physical senses. First, their hearing was influenced when the sound of a strong, gusting wind filled the house—they began to hear God-inspired sounds! Then came the appearance of fire that was seemingly magnetic in its attraction to each hungry seeker—they began to see God-inspired sights! Not only were their hearing and sight affected, but fire (which is symbolic of the Holy Spirit) then came to rest upon each one of them as they were all literally filled with the Holy Spirit. Their entire existence was saturated in God! It's no wonder that they began to speak God-inspired words!

The fire that fell from heaven divided and separated to rest upon each individual in that room. This was not a

Want More?

single flame for all to share but a God-designed, personal embrace from heaven for each one of them! Every person had an equally powerful, intimate encounter with the Holy Spirit.

They weren't Levitical high priests, nor were all Apostles. In fact, the scriptures suggest that there were one-hundred twenty people who were Spirit baptized on that morning (see Acts 1:15; 2:1). That means that ninety percent of those who received on the Day of Pentecost were not Apostles. Yet God sent His flames of fire upon every one of them because He wanted a personal, intimate encounter with each believer. Can you imagine the blessing of this intense experience? The newly baptized believers were so overjoyed, so truly drenched in God's presence and power, that some of the onlookers thought they were drunk!

The Spirit baptism brings many other personal spiritual blessings. I remember when this experience became mine. The night I received this incredible gift I followed my habit of reading the Bible before I went to bed. Something was different. It seemed as if I was wearing 3-D glasses when I read the Word, it came alive to me in such powerful new ways. And my appetite for the Bible became voracious.

My prayer life was similarly affected. I found myself getting lost in

Want More?

conversation with God. I had tried to pray for longer periods before, and it had been a real struggle. I had felt guilty that I did not enjoy prayer more. But with this new immersion in God, I found my prayer life refreshed, renewed and empowered. I was closer to God—and was enjoying Him more—than ever before.

An additional blessing was my new passion to be around other believers, listening to their testimonies and sharing with them what God had done in my life. I loved to talk about the things of God—and still do!

This immersion in God blesses us on a personal basis, yielding fruit that strengthens our lives. The book of Acts records that the newly Spirit-baptized believers

> devoted themselves to the apostles' teaching and to the fellowship, to the breaking of bread and to prayer (Acts 2:42).

Today, God wants to fulfill His word to you:

> In the last days, God says, I will pour out my Spirit on all people (Acts 2:17).

Get ready for God to pour His

Want More?

Holy Spirit upon you so that you are wonderfully drenched in Him! Won't that help satisfy your need for greater spiritual intimacy with God? But what about your hunger for greater spiritual power?

External Ministry: Greater Spiritual Power from God

While the first benefit — the personal immersion in God — is only for you, the second benefit of the Spirit baptism helps other people. God not only wants to increase your intimacy with Him but also your spiritual power to minister.

Acts 1:8 records Jesus' promise:

You will receive power when the Holy Spirit comes on you; and you will be my witnesses.

This baptism is not just for our personal spiritual blessing. It also empowers us to bless others! The baptism is not just something that happens "to me," but also something that happens "through me".

The first Pentecostal believers were sitting down when they received (see Acts 2:2), but after enjoying a season of refreshing, Peter changed his posture:

Then Peter stood up with the eleven, raised his voice and

addressed the crowd: "Fellow
Jews and all of you who live
in Jerusalem, let me explain
this to you; listen carefully to
what I say" (Acts 2:14).

After a season of personal blessing,
the 120 "receivers" on the Day of
Pentecost shared their newfound empow-
erment with others. The results were
dramatic. Three thousand were born-
again!

The first 120 were compelled to
minister because they simply could not
help overflowing! The great responsibility
that comes with the power was naturally
fulfilled as they chose to change their
posture from sit-down receivers to that of
stand-up-and-speak-out givers.

The baptism in the Spirit is the
God-powered tool of evangelism and
ministry for believers today as well. It
increases our ministry effectiveness just as
it did for the early Christians on the day
of Pentecost.

But many have received this
beautiful gift without a clear understanding of their new responsibility.

The Bible addresses this issue
clearly. Every believer carries the personal
responsibility to share his or her faith.
There are, of course, those who are called
as vocational evangelists (see Ephesians 4),
but all Christians are called to be evangel-
istic witnesses. The Spirit baptism

Want More?

empowers us to fulfill the awesome responsibility of Christ's Great Commission:

> Therefore go and make disciples of all nations, baptizing them in the name of the Father and of the Son and of the Holy Spirit, and teaching them to obey everything I have commanded you (Matthew 28:19–20a).

Want More?

For Reflection:

1. What are your greatest spiritual needs?

2. How does the Spirit baptism directly answer these needs?

3. Can you have a great spiritual experience and yet live your life no differently afterwards?

3

Who Can Receive?

As we discussed earlier, the most important event in a person's life is when he (or she) is born again, receiving Christ as his (or her) Savior. The importance of any other experience pales by comparison.

Being born again opens the doorway for all of the Kingdom benefits and blessings to flow into your life. Psalm 103:2–5 enumerates some of these benefits (while keeping the forgiveness of sin primary):

> Praise the LORD, O my soul;
> and forget not all his
> benefits—who forgives all
> your sins and heals all your
> diseases, who redeems your
> life from the pit and crowns
> you with love and compas-
> sion, who satisfies your
> desires with good things so

that your youth is renewed
like the eagle's.

God foreshadowed His Pentecost
plan throughout Scripture. From the
very beginning of creation the Holy
Spirit was moving over the waters (see
Genesis 1:2). In the Old Testament, God
selectively empowered a relatively small
number of people with His Holy Spirit.
He moved in such a way upon Moses, an
occasional judge (such as Samson or
Gideon), the prophets, and a few kings
(like Saul or David).

This anointing power, however,
was not intended to remain infrequent or
temporary. When THE Anointed One
came on the scene, He would fulfill the
old covenant and usher in a new and
better one. This new era would be
marked by the Spirit's power becoming
available to all:

In the last days, God says,
I will pour out my Spirit on
all people (Acts 2:17).

Like all post-salvation benefits,
there is only one requirement. Peter
declared that anyone who is born again is
fully qualified to receive the Spirit
baptism:

Peter replied, "Repent and be
baptized, every one of you, in

Want More?

the name of Jesus Christ for
the forgiveness of your sins.
And you will receive the gift
of the Holy Spirit"
(Acts 2:38).

I have seen children, teens, young
adults, grandparents, new converts, and
old converts receive. The qualification is
not age or spiritual maturity, but salvation.

Yet many distance themselves from
receiving because they don't feel holy
enough. They are looking at this gift
backwards. The baptism is not given as a
reward for exceptional spirituality or
holiness. It is not a merit badge you earn
by your accumulated goodness. You don't
have to become more holy to receive, but
receiving now will help you to become
more holy!

I have often heard, "You must
clean up the vessel before God can fill it."
This is true to an extent, but we must be
careful to explain from the Scriptures
what this means. When you are born
again, your sins are forgiven and you are
washed clean by Christ; as white as snow!
Your sin is no longer part of your identity
in God's eyes; your identity comes totally
from your newly adopted Father God, and
He is thoroughly holy. Though it is true
that Christians may struggle with sin
issues, they are still candidates to receive
the Spirit's power. A struggling believer

Want More?

needs His power even more!

Ask God to freshly forgive you right now. Ask Him to help you overcome temptations. The moment you ask for forgiveness you are clean.

Another parallel issue that surfaces is feeling unworthy. If you feel unworthy …GOOD! Of course we are unworthy to receive any gift from God! If we got what we deserved we'd all be in hell right now! Lamentations 3 says,

> Because of the Lord's great love we are not consumed, for his compassions never fail. They are new every morning; great is your faithfulness (Lamentations 3:22–23).

Thank God that He doesn't act according to our personal worthiness. He acts according to the worthiness that we have received by accepting Christ's sacrifice. In fact, you and I are qualified to receive God's forgiveness because we are so unworthy. Paul tells us:

> But God demonstrates his own love for us in this: While we were still sinners, Christ died for us (Romans 5:8).

If you still struggle with feelings of

Want More?

unworthiness, use them for your advantage. View them as trophies of God's grace and power in your life. When you remember something terrible that you have done, begin to thank Christ that His blood and grace have powerfully overcome that sin.

Someone once commented to me that he wished he could forget his sins altogether. I responded that it is a blessing to be able to remember our sins. If we could not remember, there would be no basis for worship or praise. We could not remember why we need Christ or truly appreciate His holiness.

We encounter what God does first, before we learn who He is. In fact, we learn who He is through what He does! We praise God because He rescued us from the sin-punishment we deserve. We worship Him because we have grown to know Him, who He is—that He is completely worthy of worship.

Now that you are born again, you are a walking trophy case of God's power over your sin, and you are fully qualified to receive the promised Spirit baptism. Get ready, your moment is almost here!

Want More?

For Reflection:

1. How does your "sense of unworthiness" affect your walk with God? Do you feel it is healthy or unhealthy?

2. If you have been struggling with sin issues, how can the Spirit baptism help?

3. Is it more important that you forget your sins or that God does?

4

How Can I Be Sure That I Have Received?

Suppose you make a purchase at a store. The clerk hands you a receipt, proving that the ownership has legally transferred from the store to you. Some stores even check the receipt before you exit the building, wanting to prove that you indeed purchased the items you are carrying! The receipt is not the purchase; it is merely the proof of the transaction.

When it comes to the question of whether you have received the baptism in the Holy Spirit, God wants to give you proof of the transaction. He wants you to be confident you have actually received the power He promised you.

There are four accounts of people actually receiving the Spirit baptism in Scripture. Three give details of how the recipients responded, proving their

Want More?

experience. One narrative, Acts 8:9–24, gives no specific details about the recipients' response—only that it was something generally observable (see verse 18).

The three detailed accounts relate one consistent proof of the Spirit baptism: the recipients began to speak in languages that they had never learned before. They began to speak in other tongues.

Let's look closer at these three occurrences.

On the Day of Pentecost:

> When the day of Pentecost came, they were all together in one place. Suddenly a sound like the blowing of a violent wind came from heaven and filled the whole house where they were sitting. They saw what seemed to be tongues of fire that separated and came to rest on each of them. All of them were filled with the Holy Spirit and **began to speak in other tongues** as the Spirit enabled them (Acts 2:1–4).

At the house of Cornelius the Gentile in Caesarea:

Want More?

> While Peter was still speaking
> these words, the Holy Spirit
> came on all who heard the
> message. The circumcised
> believers [Jews] who had come
> with Peter were astonished
> that the gift of the Holy
> Spirit had been poured out
> even on the Gentiles. For
> they heard them **speaking in
> tongues** and praising God
> (Acts 10:44–46).

In Ephesus:

> When Paul placed his hands
> on them, the Holy Spirit
> came upon them, and they
> **spoke in tongues** and
> prophesied. There were
> about twelve men in all (Acts
> 19:6–7).

The Bible is specific; when you
receive the same experience, you will have
the same proof.

Were the disciples surprised when
they began to speak in tongues on
Pentecost? Of course not. Jesus had
prepared them to expect tongues as a sign
of their belief in Him.

> And these signs will accom-
> pany those who believe: In
> my name they will drive out

demons; they will speak in
new tongues ... (Mark 16:17).

In fact, Paul repeated to the
Corinthians what Isaiah had prophesied
concerning speaking in tongues:

Through men of strange
tongues and through the lips
of foreigners I will speak to
these people ... (1 Corinthians 14:21b).

Paul explained this verse is about
speaking in tongues—or unlearned
languages.

Why?

So the big question is this: Why in
the world would God choose such a
controversial sign to prove that His Spirit
baptism had occurred?
The Scriptures give us clues into
the "why" of tongues. James, the half
brother of Jesus, records one such clue in
his epistle (letter):

All kinds of animals, birds,
reptiles and creatures of the
sea are being tamed and have
been tamed by man, but no
man can tame the tongue. It
is a restless evil, full of deadly
poison (James 3:7–8).

Want More?

James wrote his letter to believers (see James 1:1–2) and told them that they had trouble controlling their tongues. What could better demonstrate a new spiritual empowering than our tongues, previously "a restless evil," suddenly being under the influence of the Holy Spirit?

Another clue as to the "why" of tongues surfaces when we consider the "why" of the Spirit baptism itself. In essence, the baptism is all about God directing our speech in new and powerful ways so we could become ministering witnesses, as Acts 1:8 declares. This dynamic witness is demonstrated by Peter's sermon on Pentecost day. After receiving the Spirit baptism, this fisherman, who had formerly denied Christ, was empowered to speak about Him publicly to thousands!

The Spirit baptism is all about God directing and empowering our speech. You see, God wants to speak through us. It's as simple as that. I know that every time I speak in tongues, the Holy Spirit is guiding my speech. And if I can trust God to order my words in a language I do not know, how much more can I trust Him to order words in my known language? What confidence it brings to know that He will likewise guide my known language when I share Christ!

This was the Apostle Peter's explanation to the onlookers on the Day of Pentecost:

Want More?

These men are not drunk, as
you suppose. It's only nine
in the morning! No, this is
what was spoken by the prophet
Joel:

In the last days, God says,
I will pour out my Spirit
upon all people. Your sons
and daughters will prophesy.

Peter deliberately connected the
Spirit baptism with divinely guided
speech. He said in essence, "Why does
this surprise you? This is what happens
when the Spirit comes on people: they
speak forth words from God!" The word
prophesy means to "speak forth from
God".

Peter went on to explain that this
new outpouring was now available to all
believers, "all flesh".

The best clue for the "why" of
tongues is simply because the Word says
so. Aside from the narrative accounts in
Acts we've already covered, the Apostle
Paul emphatically commands:

I would like every one of you
to speak with other tongues
(1 Corinthians 14:5),

and

Want More?

> Therefore, my brothers, be
> eager to prophesy, and do not
> forbid speaking in tongues
> (1 Corinthians 14:39).

Remember that Jesus matter-of-factly told us that a sign following true believers would be speaking in tongues:

> And these signs will
> accompany those who believe
> ...they will speak with new
> tongues (Mark 16:17).

So, just like Christians in the Book of Acts, we can anticipate that we will begin to speak in unlearned languages (tongues) as proof of the baptism in the Holy Spirit. Our speech patterns will evidence Spirit-on-flesh as we begin to speak forth God-inspired words. Our divinely transformed words will then confirm our newly empowered ability to communicate Jesus to others. But will anything else—can anything else happen?

What About Emotions?

Each of us are wired very differently regarding our emotions. Some can't even watch a commercial for a *Little House on the Prairie* re-run without crying. Others have the limited emotional response of a boat anchor. Likewise, our emotional responses will be

different when we receive the baptism—
and that's okay. Don't let emotion—or
lack of emotion—override the proven,
scriptural proof of the experience. And
please realize that while the emotional
degree from person to person may vary,
the spiritual quality of the experience is
the same.

While ministering in Kansas
several years ago, I noticed a young lady
trying to receive the baptism after a
Sunday morning church service. I
approached her at the front of the
auditorium, near the altar, and asked how
she was doing. She told me she was
growing discouraged because the baptism
was not coming very easily. I talked with
her about emotional responses, that
everyone is different. She seemed
encouraged by this, but felt she wanted to
continue seeking on another occasion,
perhaps at home.

Later, after the evening service, I
saw the young woman at the altar area
again. I made my way over to her and
asked her if she wanted to try again for
the baptism. She responded, "I don't need
to try again. I received at home this
afternoon." She went on to explain that
she had always assumed people needed
some overwhelming feeling of power—or
emotional "sparkles," as she put it—in
order to receive. She decided just to ask
God and then receive. So she did! Her
experience was simple and real, but not as

emotionally overwhelming as she had anticipated.

However, I should include one more word about emotions: Don't be scared of them either! Many have been told from their youngest days to "stop crying" and "big kids don't cry." Consequently, the emotional responses of a generation have been suppressed. There are those who have become such stoics that they identify any emotional response as a weakness or liability.

Who made your emotions? Who formed you as a complete package? Our Creator-Father. There can be no more healthy, appropriate, or safe time to allow emotional responses than in His presence. Don't be afraid of going overboard or "losing control".

When I was growing up in church, we weren't afraid of emotion. We didn't even think we had a decent service until we had run out of tissues! These were the days before waterproof mascara. The ladies would leave church with black "Lone Ranger" eyes from wiping away their tears!

So many try to suppress tears when God moves upon them. Why would you try to undermine what God is doing in your life? People declare, "I'm not a crier," and then they have to prove this by trying their hardest to fight back the tears!

Let me say it again. God made your

emotions, so don't be afraid of them. However, let me also say that you shouldn't count them as a necessity either during or following the baptism of the Holy Spirit. The proof of that experience is that you will speak in an unlearned language. Be confident. You will speak in tongues; you might or might not cry.

Who's in Charge?

There is another very important underlying purpose behind speaking in tongues. You and I like to be in control. That's right; I'm a self-admitted control freak.

Partly because of our control issues, we all have drawn a line, or boundary, around our lives. This line divides what are acceptable and unacceptable behaviors for us. We could call this encircling line "our perceived dignity". Inside the line we can safely exist, not bringing unwanted shame and ridicule upon ourselves. Outside of the line lies certain humiliation.

Have you ever had a terribly embarrassing moment? (I've had more than my share!) Were these awful moments something that we purposefully arranged? Did we desire to be publicly humiliated? Of course not! No one likes to be perceived as undignified or foolish.

Our line of perceived dignity is usually crossed only by accident. However, there are rare emergencies in which we purposely override the dignity line's demarcation.

Dignity. Could this be a ploy used by our ancient enemy? Could this be the source of Lucifer's fall from heaven? The problem that caused the Fall of man?

You guessed it—dignity may often be the nice and acceptable word we use for pride. Our need to impress others and yet be perceived as "normal" stems from pride.

All of the works of God in our lives are an absolute affront to our... dignity? Let's call it what it is: PRIDE! And pride is a highly dangerous thing.

We talked earlier about how we need the Holy Spirit to convict or reveal our need for God's forgiveness. Why do we need this convicting help? Our pride says, "I'm all right. I can't admit I need an invisible God's help. I'd look weak. No, it's too embarrassing!" You can see that pride is often our worst enemy, opposing a right relationship with God.

It is no different with the Holy Spirit baptism. We must willfully abandon our pride and dignity in order to receive.

Tongues are a total assault on our pride. We don't have a clue what we are saying, only that we are speaking strange sounds. And unless someone happens to understand the language (or if it is interpreted), no one knows what we are

Want More?

saying but God! The Apostle Paul told the Corinthians:

> For if I pray in a tongue, my spirit prays, but my mind is unfruitful (1 Corinthians 14:14),

and

> For anyone who speaks in a tongue does not speak to men but to God. Indeed, no one understands him; he utters mysteries with his spirit (1 Corinthians 14:2).

You must be willing to compromise your dignity in order to receive this gift from God. You have to be willing to humble yourself, even to the point of appearing foolish and undignified.

I believe that God chose tongues to be the proof of the Spirit baptism because it directly confronts our pride and control issues. In order to receive something new from God, we must be willing to do something new for God.

Want More?

For Reflection:

1. What do you feel is the significance of speaking in tongues as proof of the Spirit baptism?

2. What role can emotion play in a healthy spiritual life? How emotionally open are you to God?

3. Do you think that your dignity has a positive or negative effect upon your walk with God?

5

How Do I Receive?

Before we begin to discuss "how you receive," let me assure you that God wants to baptize you in His Holy Spirit today! He desires to refresh and empower your life. He wants to fulfill His promise to you, so be encouraged.

Realize That It Is a Free Gift

This point cannot be overstated. The apostle Peter said the Spirit baptism was a gift (see Acts 2:38), and you can't earn free gifts.

What did you do to earn the right to receive birthday gifts? You just happened to show up on a specific day. Why should you get a gift for that? (If it were based on earning, didn't your mom do all the work? In that case, shouldn't you be sending her a gift on your birthday?)

Want More?

A few months ago, we were ministering in Arizona on the Spirit baptism. That night I prayed with a gentleman who was repeatedly begging God to baptize him. "God, if you'll just fill me, I'll stop kicking the dog when I get mad. I promise I'll try harder." He was arguing like an attorney trying to convince a judge of his case.

The desire to change is fantastic, but it won't earn the baptism. Remember, it is a free gift. And you don't need to convince God to give it to you. He already knows your need for the Spirit baptism—far more than you do! He has already decided to baptize you.

Realize What to Expect and What to Do

We talked earlier about the disciples not walking blindly into the Spirit baptism. Jesus had told them what to expect, and they anticipated it happening. In the same way, the Bible sets forth a simple pattern that helps us anticipate what will happen next as we seek to receive this gift.

In the detailed Acts accounts (see Acts 2, 10 and 19), this simple pattern emerges. It will happen in your life also, as you begin to receive this gift.

Want More?

1. Pursue Jesus

First, the seekers were obediently pursuing Jesus when they received. (Remember, Jesus is the only one who can baptize you in the Holy Spirit.)

In Acts chapter two, the followers of Jesus had waited in Jerusalem and were continually in the temple praising God, obeying the words of Christ (see also Luke 24:53).

In Acts chapter ten, the Caesarean gentiles obeyed God by calling for Peter and listening to his teaching about Jesus.

In Acts chapter 19, the new Ephesian Christians were hungry to grow in their relationship with Jesus. Paul led them to the next logical step and they received the Spirit baptism.

The rules haven't changed. If you are truly hungry, you will begin to pursue Jesus. There are many Christians who are frustrated with their spiritual lives but will do nothing to initiate change. The answer to their thirst for more spiritual intimacy and power is to seek Jesus as the Baptizer in the Holy Spirit.

I've heard it said many times this way, "You can have as much of Christ in your life as you want—and in fact, right now you do!" If we truly wanted more, we would already be pursuing it right now. So how do you pursue Jesus? Set aside some special time to talk with Him. Open up your mouth and speak words of love and worship to Him. Fellowship with Him.

If you desire to be baptized in the Holy Spirit, you must first pursue Jesus.

2. The Holy Spirit Will Then Come Upon You

Something powerful happens when we fellowship with Jesus, desiring Him to baptize us in the Holy Spirit. The Scriptures repeatedly demonstrate that God responds to our pursuit of Him.

> If my people, who are called by my name, will humble themselves and pray and seek my face and turn from their wicked ways, then I will hear from heaven and will forgive their sins and will heal their land (2 Chronicles 7:14).

> Anyone who comes to him [God] must believe that he exists and that he rewards those who earnestly seek him (Hebrews 11:6).

> Come near to God and he will come near to you (James 4:8).

> If we confess our sins, he is faithful and just and will

63

Want More?

> forgive us our sins and purify
> us from all unrighteousness
> (1 John 1:9).

> I [Jesus] stand at the door and
> knock. If anyone hears my
> voice and opens the door, I
> will come in (Revelation
> 3:20).

This principle applies to every transaction we have with God. He has given us freedom to choose our destiny. When we choose Him, He responds to us.

How does this apply to the Spirit baptism? When we pursue Jesus as the Baptizer in the Holy Spirit, He will respond to us!

How did He respond to those in Scripture who were seeking the baptism?

> Suddenly a sound like the
> blowing of a violent wind
> came from heaven and filled
> the whole house where they
> were sitting. They saw what
> seemed to be tongues of fire
> that separated and came to
> rest on each one of them
> (Acts 2:2–3).

> While Peter was still speaking
> these words, the Holy Spirit
> came on all who heard the
> message (Acts 10:44).

Want More?

When Paul placed his hands
on them, the Holy Spirit
came on them (Acts 19:6a).

As the believers in Acts pursued
Jesus, He sent the Holy Spirit to come
upon them.

This word "upon" has distinct
meaning. In all of the accounts of Spirit
baptism in Scripture, the Greek verb "epi"
is used. It means "to come upon," though
it is sometimes translated simply as "on".

Since every believer is the temple of
the Holy Spirit (see 1 Corinthians 3:16)
and each one has the Spirit living in him
or her (see Romans 8:9), the coming
"upon" of the Spirit has a different
meaning.

Jesus said to those who followed
Him, "You will receive power when the
Holy Spirit comes on you" (Acts 1:8).

God's response to our seeking the
baptism is that the Holy Spirit's power
will come upon us!

You can take that to the bank. If
you begin to pursue Jesus, you will
suddenly sense the Spirit is coming upon
you. This will happen in every case
because God's will is to baptize every
believer in the Holy Spirit!

How Will I Know?

You might ask, "How will I know

when the Holy Spirit comes upon me?" There is no specific measurement of "voltage" that will hit you. In fact, many are surprised by the gentleness and beauty of the Spirit's touch.

But some get into God's presence and begin to hyper-analyze everything, moving their attention from seeking God to their subjective appraisals. "I think I feel God. I kind of feel a warmth — then again, I am wearing a sweater! I feel a bit weak in the knees; maybe I'm going to fall over — then again, I do have bad knees and I have been standing for a while." The analysis begins and the focus shifts.

If you are pursuing Jesus by asking Him to reveal Himself as the Baptizer in the Holy Spirit, and you begin to sense His indefinable presence descend on you, be confident that He is answering your prayer.

You may have an emotional or even a physical response. Perhaps you will sense Him drawing near. In any event, you will suddenly be aware of His presence in a manner that was not there just a moment before. Be assured, your moment has come!

3. Cooperate with the Holy Spirit by Speaking Out

What do you do when you sense the Holy Spirit coming upon you? Do what the hungry believers in Acts did!

Want More?

All of them were filled with
the Holy Spirit and began to
speak in other tongues as the
Spirit enabled them (Acts
2:4).

For they [Peter and his Jewish
friends] heard them
[Cornelius and the other
gentiles] speaking in tongues
and praising God (Acts
10:46).

When Paul placed his hands
on them, the Holy Spirit
came on them, and they
spoke in tongues and
prophesied (Acts 19:6).

When the Spirit came upon them,
the Acts recipients cooperated with the
Holy Spirit, choosing to speak out in
tongues as He enabled them.

But who actually speaks in the
unknown tongue? Every reference to
speaking in tongues in the Bible tells us
that the person did the physical speaking—not the Spirit. The Holy Spirit
doesn't speak in tongues, but He gives
people the ability to do so. (After all, to
the Omniscient Spirit no language can be
unknown.) We do the speaking, but He
gives the script.

Remember, this is a process of

cooperation between the Holy Spirit and the believer. The supernatural part of the process is that the Holy Spirit is enabling the words that are being spoken. The natural part is the physical act of speaking itself; that part is up to you.

Many people struggle with this point. They say, "I want it to be all God and not me." That is an impossible desire. God doesn't want to do it by Himself; He wants to partner with you!

Some eliminate the opportunity for cooperation with the Spirit by their fear of "being in the flesh". They forget that "flesh" is exactly the raw material God desires to work with:

> In the last days, God says,
> I will pour out my Spirit on
> all people (Acts 2:17).

The word translated as "people" is really the word for "flesh" in the original Greek. God wants to partner His supernatural strength with our fleshly weakness!

As the Spirit came upon the seeking believers, they began to speak in other languages. The Holy Spirit did not force them to speak; they chose to cooperate and speak His words.

Some make the mistake of thinking that the Holy Spirit will seize control of their jaw, vocal chords and tongue. Remember, it is an act of divine coopera-

Want More?

tion. You choose to partner your speech with the Holy Spirit's utterance. Your voice will not change; you will not be "out of control".

So this simple pattern is evident in all three detailed Acts narratives:

1. Pursue Jesus; seek and worship Him.
2. The Holy Spirit will then come upon you.
3. You must cooperate with the Spirit by beginning to speak as He enables you.

The Two Paths

What is our natural response to the Holy Spirit? We resist Him. Our default response is trying to stay in control.

Here is a simple principle that has helped many to understand their responsibility in receiving: When the Holy Spirit comes upon you, you are suddenly confronted with a fork in the road. What will you do? Which of the two paths will you follow?

The Easy Path: Stay in the Comfort Zone

The easiest path to take is the path of the familiar by following your own understanding. Your control and dignity are still intact; you are not doing anything perceived as risky.

Picture this: We are pursuing Jesus by intimately worshipping and fellowshipping with Him, and then the Spirit comes upon us. What do we do now? We naturally continue doing what we were doing and saying what we were saying before He came upon us. This way we are still in control. Everything is safe and comfortable. What will most likely happen? Probably nothing, because we are not cooperating with the Holy Spirit!

Do nothing different and you will automatically follow this pathway by default. If you do what you've always done, you will remain where you've always been. Receiving something new requires a new action.

The Right Path: Take a Leap of Faith

When the Holy Spirit comes upon you, there is another path you can follow. This path leads far away from your comfort zone. This way is chosen when you want more of God and decide to step out in faith and trust Him. His promises are always true. You will be safe!

If you choose to take the leap of faith, you will most likely feel self-conscious and vulnerable. This proves that the line of dignity is being crossed. Don't worry now. Jesus can't wait to baptize you in the Holy Spirit!

Want More?

Jump!

What do we mean by the "leap of faith"?

God gave me a simple explanation for faith: faith is a teaspoon of understanding and a swimming pool full of trust. Since you cannot baptize yourself in the Spirit, you must trust God and His promise enough to do something risky— something outside the lines of dignity, something that is an act of raw trust.

When our son Dolan was three years old, he and I would play a little game. He needed help with tying his shoes. I would pick him up, sit him on the kitchen counter, then tie his shoe-laces. When finished, I'd take a step back and extend my arms toward him, encouraging him to jump. Dolan would give me one of his million-dollar smiles, along with a few giggles, as he took a daring leap into my arms.

He depended upon my strength to catch him. As his dad, I wouldn't even consider not catching him!

The same principle operates in receiving the Spirit baptism. Jesus put it this way:

> Which of you fathers, if your son asks for a fish, will give him a snake instead? Or if he asks for an egg, will give him

a scorpion? If you then,
though you are evil, know
how to give good gifts to
your children, how much
more will your Father in
heaven give the Holy Spirit
to those who ask him (Luke
11:11–13)?

When the Holy Spirit comes upon
you, it is God's way of saying, "It's Me.
It's safe. Jump into My arms!"

I've heard it said that the safest
place you can ever be is where you are
receiving from God. He will not let you
fall; remember, from the moment you are
born again, it is His will to baptize you in
the Spirit (see Acts 2:38–39). You will
not get a counterfeit when you seek to
receive this promise from Jesus, the
Baptizer. The Father guarantees His
work. He is going to catch you!

How to Take the Leap of Faith

Are you wondering how to take the
required leap of faith? God's Word speaks
to this clearly: When the Spirit baptizes
us, He will give us the ability to speak in
unlearned languages. They may be
human languages or heavenly ones (see 1
Corinthians 13:1), but you will not
understand what you are saying.

The moment He comes upon you,
He will help you—if you take a leap of

faith and begin to speak out. If you sense the Spirit coming upon you and then stop welcoming His power by ceasing to speak, the miracle will be delayed.

You see, yielding is the catalyst in receiving from God. Many think of yielding as a passive act, just waiting around. "Lord, I'm just standing here yielding to you until you do something to me."

But yielding is active, not passive. If you are trying to surrender to an opposing army, do you just wait for them to find you? No, you wave your white flag and find them, insuring your intentions are clear. Yielding is an action of surrender and cooperation.

The leap of faith is actively yielding your speech to the direction of the Holy Spirit.

We talked earlier about the simple pattern that emerges in the detailed Acts accounts:

1. Pursue Jesus; seek and worship Him.
2. The Holy Spirit will then come upon you.
3. Cooperate with the Spirit by beginning to speak out the unlearned language as He enables you.

The first step is up to you, something you must initiate. The second step

Want More?

is something that only God can initiate. The third step is a cooperative effort between you and God, your voice speaking His words.

Remember the fork in the road? When the Holy Spirit comes upon you, it is your choice to continue in your own understanding or to take a leap of faith into your Father's arms, trusting His promise to enable you to speak in unlearned languages. Will you trust God enough to open your mouth and speak words that you will not understand?

Now, fasten your seatbelt. It's time to receive!

Want More?

For Reflection:

1. Why do you think we try to earn things from God?

2. Have you ever sensed the Holy Spirit coming upon you?

3. How does Luke 11:11-13 strengthen our courage that we will indeed receive a genuine experience?

6

Receive Now!

It's time to put into practice what we have learned. It's your turn to personally experience Jesus Christ as YOUR Baptizer in the Holy Spirit.

The following steps are a helpful guide in receiving, but remember: Jesus can't wait to baptize you in His Holy Spirit. You might not make it through all the steps before you receive!

Some Practical Helps

Turn off the outside distractions. Get alone and shut the door. Sometimes people who have sought to receive for many years in church really just need to be alone for this part. When we are alone, the risk of feeling embarrassed or self-conscious is diminished.

If you feel as though you need someone to join you in prayer, that's fine.

Want More?

Just make sure you can together seek the Lord in an uninhibited way.

Block out some time to worship and seek Jesus. You must intentionally pursue Him.

Read the following verses to reassure you and build faith: Acts 1:4–8; 2:1–18.

One More Thing!

Decide now that you will indeed take the leap of faith when you sense the Holy Spirit coming upon you. Decide now that you will open your mouth and speak, trusting the Holy Spirit to give you the strange, new words.

Since you only have one mouth, you can only speak in one language at a time. This means English or other learned languages will have to go, or they will crowd out the spiritual language. When He comes upon you, resist the urge for English to dominate. The Bible clearly tells us that we will speak in NEW languages, not KNOWN languages (Acts 2:4). Refuse the known language and speak out. It's safe; God will keep His promise to you.

Choose now to stop allowing your brain to rule your mouth. Get ready to open up and speak, trusting the Holy Spirit to prompt you with new words.

These unfamiliar words are God's confirmation that you have received this

Want More?

beautiful gift.

Just as a skydiver must prepare to jump from an airplane before his feet ever leave the ground, you must now decide to actually jump into your Father's arms when He gives the signal! Don't allow fear of the unknown to keep you on the plane; you will receive a genuine experience. God promised this gift to you, and He is faithful.

Here We Go!

Now you're in the secret place, ready to receive. I encourage you to read through these simple steps first, to see where we are going. Then follow the instructions as you read them a second time. Here we go!

1. Ask Jesus for a fresh cleansing from any unconfessed sin.

   (Notice I said unconfessed. You don't need to dig through the history books and re-confess your guilt over forgiven sins. Remember, guilt comes from the enemy but conviction comes from the Holy Spirit.) Look into your heart. Are you struggling with anger or bitterness? Ask God to help you forgive those who are hurting you. Ask Him to forgive your current sins.

Want More?

2. Confess your dependence on Jesus.

    Take a few minutes and allow
    yourself to realize how much you
    truly need Him. Tell Him how
    much your life depends on Him.
    Let Him know that you trust Him
    and welcome all that He has for
    you.

3. Ask Jesus to baptize you in His
    Holy Spirit.

    Invite Christ to reveal
    Himself as your Baptizer in the
    Holy Spirit. Don't beg; just ask.
    He already desires to fill you; He
    doesn't need convincing. Ask a few
    times, telling Him how hungry you
    are for new spiritual intimacy and
    empowerment. Tell Him that you
    will accept His promise right now.

4. Begin to open your mouth and
    speak praise and thanks to Jesus.

    Do not ask anymore; He has
    heard you. Even if you are quiet
    and timid, lift your voice and bless
    Him out loud. Get used to hearing
    your voice praise Jesus. That's the
    highest form of human speech!
    Tell Him how much the cross
    means to you. Tell Him how much

you love Him. Thank Him that you don't have to go to hell anymore. You don't have to be poetic; don't try to impress Him with your words. Jesus loves you and knows your heart. Be yourself and praise Him out loud!

You will, at some point, begin to run out of words. This is okay; just keep speaking praise and thanks out loud to Him. Get creative. Don't just repeat one word or phrase over and over. Express your thanks, telling Him from the depths of your heart what He means to you.

5. When the Holy Spirit comes upon you, let go of English and speak out.

When the Spirit comes upon you, you will NOT be out of control or in some sort of "out of body" state, but you will probably feel like your mouth wants to say something. Now is the time to jump into your Heavenly Father's arms! Trust the Spirit, not the brain. Refuse to speak the known language and trust the enablement of the Spirit. He will not let you down; He will put new words in your mouth as you speak.

God does not seize control

Want More?

and force you to start talking, you must choose to speak out boldly when His Spirit is upon you. Sometimes people sense strange, new words in their heart as the Spirit comes upon them. Often people do not know what they are to say until after they hear themselves speak in tongues. God can give the words in any way He chooses! Be assured, the Holy Spirit will enable you to speak His words.

You may stammer at first. That's all right; keep on speaking. Don't retreat to the safety zone of known language.

Continue to trust God and more will come. Some find singing in tongues flows easier for them. That's fine. Do what feels spiritually natural.

Be confident. The words you are speaking or singing are from God; they are not from you or the Devil. Remember Jesus' assurance that we will not have a counterfeit experience:

> Which of you fathers, if your son asks for a fish, will give him a snake instead? Or if he asks for an egg, will give him a scorpion? If you then, though you

81

Want More?

are evil, know how to
give good gifts to your
children, how much
more will your Father
in heaven give the
Holy Spirit to those
who ask him (Luke
11:11–13)?

You asked Jesus to baptize
you, so this is the work of Christ!
Don't be shocked if you do
not experience overwhelming
emotion. The proof is in the
language, not the tears.

6. Thank Jesus for baptizing you,
then begin to speak out in the
spiritual language again.

You have now been baptized
in the Holy Spirit. You have the
same, biblical proof that the
Apostles and early Christians
experienced.
You can speak in tongues
whenever you pray or worship. It is
now a built-in component of your
spiritual life:

For if I pray in a
tongue, my spirit prays,
but my mind is un-
fruitful. So what shall
I do? I will pray with

Want More?

my spirit, but I will also
pray with my mind; I
will sing with my spirit,
but I will also sing with
my mind (1 Corin-
thians 14:14–15).

Want More?

For Reflection:

1. I encourage you to write the date below. This will serve as a record of your wonderful experience.

   I received the baptism in the Holy Spirit on_____.
   (date)

   I have experienced the biblical evidence of speaking in unlearned tongues, just like the early Christians.

2. Tell someone else what just happened to you.

7

What in the World Just Happened to Me?

You did it! You jumped into your Father's arms and He caught you!

You may feel a bit self-conscious as you look back at your experience. That's normal. You were doing something new, something that made you vulnerable.

If you have only a few words (or even one word), keep speaking what He has given to you. God is generous. More will come. Enjoy your newfound spiritual language, and explore your new vocabulary. He has a lifetime of words for you.

What About Fear and Doubts?

Many Christians experience fear and doubts after great spiritual victories. Our adversary uses these same weapons repeatedly, but they don't have to work against you. James tells us,

Want More?

Submit yourselves, then,
to God. Resist the Devil,
and he will flee from you
(James 4:7).

So resist him and he will go!

Fears and doubts also naturally arise after any new experience, simply because we have not acclimated to the "new normal".

You may be tempted to think, "That was just me." Of course it was you—your voice speaking God's words, words that we aren't supposed to understand! Don't forget that you took Jesus at His word. He promised you would speak in new tongues. This is solidly biblical and proves that He now will likewise guide your known language to minister to others.

Your experience was real. You are now newly empowered by the Holy Spirit, but there are still a few things you need to know.

Want More?

For Reflection:

1. Did you feel self-conscious as you took the leap of faith and began to speak in tongues? If so, why?

2. What is a practical step you can take to overcome doubts and fears (James 4:7)?

Want More?

8

How Can I Stay Full of the Holy Spirit and His Power?

You have spent time reading this book because you are hungry for more of the Holy Spirit's ministry and power in your life. Don't quit the quest now!

You have been newly immersed in God and empowered by Him for ministry. He has also added a new dimension to your prayer life. Your new ability to speak in tongues is now a standard feature of your spiritual walk. Although tongues function as evidence, they have several other roles in a believer's life; all of which can help you stay full of the Holy Spirit's power.

Two Types of Tongues

The Scriptures show that there is a place for tongues in our private devotional life and also a place in public

Want More?

worship.

Though the emphasis of this book is on the Spirit baptism and the accompanying devotional tongues, let's look quickly at the difference between public and devotional tongues.

Tongues in public worship fall under the nine manifestation gifts of the Holy Spirit (see 1 Corinthians 12:4–11). Although they may sound the same, public tongues serve a different purpose from devotional tongues. In 1 Corinthians 14, Paul lists three requirements for tongues in public worship:

1. Public tongues require the attention of the congregation (see verse 5).
2. Public tongues require an interpretation in a known language (see verse 27).
3. Public tongues must edify or encourage the congregation (see verse 5).

When you are baptized in the Spirit, you do not have to speak in tongues publicly. The direction to speak a public utterance in tongues is a distinct, purposeful compulsion that the Holy Spirit gives on specific occasions.

This is clearly different from your private, devotional language, which is between you and God. Scripture recounts other characteristics for devotional

Want More?

tongues:

1. Devotional tongues require Spirit baptism (see Acts 2:4).
2. Devotional tongues do not require interpretation in a known language (see Acts 10:46).
3. Devotional tongues will edify or encourage your personal life (see 1 Corinthians 14:4).

Because speaking in unlearned languages is the first sign that you have been baptized in the Holy Spirit, there is the tendency to leave it there and forget the need to speak in devotional tongues on a daily basis. Speaking in tongues is an essential part of your new life of walking in the Spirit and will help you stay full of the Holy Spirit.

Why Should I Speak in Tongues Every Day?

There are at least four reasons that we absolutely need to speak in tongues every day.

1. **Speaking in tongues daily is essential because it expresses worship.**

On the day of Pentecost, the attentive onlookers understood the tongues spoken by the first Charismatics as worship:

> We hear them declaring the wonders of God in our own tongues (Acts 2:11).

At Cornelius's house, the Jews also recognized tongues as an expression of worship:

> For they heard them speaking in tongues and praising God (Acts 10:46).

Haven't you been frustrated on occasion with your worship? Haven't you run out of words that can express who God is and how much He means to you? The language of the Spirit is there to express perfect worship. Thank God!

2. **Speaking in tongues daily is essential because it expresses effective intercession.**

(Intercession is just a fancy word for praying for others.) You quickly discover how needy you are when you try to pray. In fact, prayer is a declaration of our weakness and God's ability!

Paul told the Roman church that the Holy Spirit would aid our intercession:

Want More?

> In the same way, the Spirit
> helps us in our weakness. We
> do not know what we ought
> to pray for, but the Spirit
> himself intercedes for us with
> groans that words cannot
> express. And he who
> searches our hearts knows the
> mind of the Spirit, because
> the Spirit intercedes for the
> saints in accordance with
> God's will (Romans 8:26–27).

In 1 Corinthians 14:15, Paul encourages us to pray both in tongues and in our known languages, identifying two types of intercession.

The first type of intercession flows from our understanding. For example, you hear about a big need and feel moved to pray. You begin to pray out of your understanding of the need. Your intellect forms the word petitions to God.

The second type of intercession flows from God's understanding. He moves us to pray, but we don't know what we ought to pray for or how we should pray—so we pray in tongues. Paul said,

> The Spirit searches all things,
> even the deep things of God.
> For who among man knows
> the thoughts of a man except
> the man's spirit within him?

Want More?

In the same way no one
knows the thoughts of God
except the Spirit of God (1
Corinthians 2:10b–11).

When we intercede in tongues, we
are praying with God's intelligence! We
are safe inside His perfect will!

3. Speaking in tongues daily is
essential because it expresses the
mystery of the divine.

There is a tension between the
natural and the supernatural from our
vantage point. We occupy natural bodies
in a natural world, but we have spiritual
needs and spiritual appetites. Often we
wish that God's realm were easier to
understand.

The supernatural cannot be
reconciled by the natural mind. All of
our tidy outlines and flowcharts can't
contain the mystery of God and His plan,
so our understanding hits a brick wall.

No, we speak of God's secret
wisdom, a wisdom that has
been hidden and that God
destined for our glory before
time began. However, as it is
written: "No eye has seen, no
ear has heard, no mind has
conceived what God has
prepared for those who love

Want More?

him" but God has revealed it
to us by his Spirit (1 Corinthians 2:9–10a).

The only way you can understand
spiritual truth is when it is spiritually
revealed. God's Spirit reveals to us what
we need to understand.

How does this factor into speaking
in tongues? God has given us the ability
to begin to speak in spiritual words
whenever we need to do so. We stand on
the natural side of the Grand Canyon of
mystery and God stands on the distant
supernatural side. However, speaking in
tongues builds a bridge across that
mysterious chasm that separates the two
realms. Whenever we are afraid or
confused, or we don't understand what
God desires, we can choose to lower the
drawbridge from our side by speaking in
the spiritual language He has given us!

Sometimes our willingness to trust
God and speak in tongues will also result
in faith-building bridges between others.
A Pennsylvania pastor related this story
to me recently concerning my wife's
brother, Doug, who is a missionary to the
nation of Indonesia.

While raising his support, Doug
had ministered at this pastor's rural
church in Pennsylvania. After Doug's
presentation of Indonesia's great spiritual
need, he called the congregation to pray
for the Indonesian people. The congrega-

tion stepped forward and quietly began to
kneel and pray around the altar area in
front of the platform. Doug was also
praying while walking around the altar
area.

As he walked, he could hear
different people praying, and one
woman's prayer suddenly caught his
attention. Discreetly, Doug asked the
pastor to come with him to speak to her.
When he did so, Doug asked the woman
if she had ever traveled abroad. She said
no. He asked her if she knew anyone
overseas. She again answered in the
negative. He asked her if she had ever
studied a foreign language. This time,
when she said no, Doug began to relate
the miracle.

She was praying perfectly in an
Indonesian dialect!

She had been unsure what specifi-
cally to pray about and so was praying in
tongues. The language of the Spirit
lowered the drawbridge over that
mysterious chasm and connected with
God's power—not only for this woman
but also for Doug and the entire congregation.

At that moment, the details of
"how" didn't matter. There was spiritual
revelation. They all knew that God was
going to do a mighty work in Indonesia!

When you can't figure out how to
reach God, when you don't know how to
pray, let the language of the Spirit express

the mystery and build the bridge to God.

4. Speaking in tongues daily is essential because it expresses confidence.

We talked earlier about tongues edifying or encouraging you spiritually. Jude verse 20 reinforces this:

> But you, dear friends, build
> yourselves up in your most
> holy faith and pray in the
> Holy Spirit.

Yet there is another way tongues express spiritual confidence on our part. Do you remember why tongues are essential to the Holy Spirit baptism? One of many reasons we discussed is purpose oriented. The true fulfillment of the Spirit baptism is empowered speech to minister. Remember, if we can speak in the unknown language as the Spirit guides us, how much more can we depend on Him to guide our known language when we share Christ! When you speak in tongues, you are expressing confidence that God is going to powerfully guide your next ministry opportunity.

Speaking in the unknown tongue is a wonderful way to daily stay full of the Holy Spirit. Your unknown spiritual language will express worship, intercession, mystery and confidence. Praise God

Want More?

for His incredible gift!

Want More?

For Reflection:

1. How do the two types of tongues differ in purpose and function?

2. What specific ways do you think speaking in tongues on a daily basis will enhance your spiritual life?

3. Try out your new gift as a part of your devotions today!

9

How Can I Let the Power Out?

Before I received the Spirit baptism, I had never led anyone to the Lord. I was scared to death at the thought of even trying, but I also felt an immense amount of guilt because I was failing at my responsibility to be a witness.

After I received the baptism on that wonderful August evening, everything changed. My spiritual appetites increased because my intimacy with God grew. The spiritual power that I had longed for was now within reach. But witnessing? I wasn't so sure of that!

Then, only a few days after receiving, it happened to me. I met a person "accidentally" who was really struggling. She tried to put on the everything-is-all-right act, but I could tell something was wrong.

Up to this time my only reference

point for sharing my faith was knocking on doors to distribute gospel tracts. (We would ring the doorbell and pray that no one answered!) Suddenly something was different. While I was still somewhat apprehensive and fearful, I found myself saying the right things. In fact, the words were so right that I knew they were not coming from my brain! God was truly guiding my known language just as He had recently guided me to speak in the unknown language. It was working!

In just a few moments, I was leading my friend in a prayer, and she was accepting Christ as her Savior! I felt like I had won a million dollars! Yet the celebration wasn't only going on in my life. There was celebration in heaven also:

> In the same way, I tell you, there is rejoicing in the presence of the angels of God over one sinner who repents (Luke 15:10).

It was so easy, so natural. I couldn't help overflowing!

Stagnant Ponds

This overflowing is supremely important. Have you ever seen a stagnant pond? Don't let the tranquil surface fool you; the water is polluted!

Why are stagnant ponds polluted?

Want More?

Don't they receive fresh water every time it rains?

These ponds are stagnant because they have no outlet.

Their condition parallels the potential danger of those who receive the Spirit baptism and then refuse to minister to others. They stagnate. Their rivers of living water turn into a polluted pond.

Don't be like them. Share the blessing.

Some Receive Easily!

My wife, Rochelle, and I were holding one of our Holy Spirit Conferences in the Mid-west some time ago. One of the attendees, a brand-new Christian, expressed her desire to receive the Spirit baptism after one of the sessions. We prayed with her, and she experienced Jesus as the Baptizer in the Holy Spirit almost immediately. I shared with her briefly about how God would guide her speech to minister—if she would make the effort to open up her mouth around people who needed Jesus.

The next night of the conference, I asked if anyone had a testimony. She immediately hopped up and excitedly told the people how she had received the baptism the previous night. She went on to explain how I had encouraged her that God would also guide her known language if she would talk to people who didn't know Christ.

She had decided to give it a try. Earlier that day, within only a few hours of receiving the gift herself, she had won both her neighbors and nearly all the ladies in the local Laundromat to Jesus!

I watched a room full of "stagnant ponds" slide down in their chairs from embarrassment. This new believer "got it"! She had chosen to let the power out.

Now it's your turn. You have been baptized in the Holy Spirit. God has given you the powerful ability to speak in tongues. Where will you go from here?

Don't Forget to Take Him Home

I recall traveling through Lancaster County, Pennsylvania some years ago. Many Amish people live there and they practice strict religious ideals. They have chosen to reject modern discoveries and inventions such as automobiles and electricity for personal use. However, they enjoy these conveniences in public places. In fact, if you ever visit the Wal-Mart in Lancaster, you will find a special parking area for Amish horses and buggies. They choose to shop at Wal-Mart for items manufactured in factories and delivered by trucks to a store built by engines and powered by electricity. Interesting.

While driving through the Lancaster countryside, I passed one

Want More?

Amish farm after another, and I began to notice a gray line consistently appearing on each one of their roofs. Curious, I looked up and realized that it was the shadow of the power lines that ran overhead—unconnected power lines.

The Amish have chosen to allow electricity to influence certain areas of their lives, but they don't take it home with them. The very same electricity that they enjoy in Wal-Mart is available twenty feet from their rooftops, but it never gets inside their homes.

In this way the Amish are not unlike those Spirit baptized believers who enjoy wonderful moves of the Spirit in their churches—but they don't take Him home.

Please don't forget the choice that is yours to make every time you encounter someone who doesn't know Jesus. You can either choose to open your mouth and allow the power to flow, or you can keep your mouth shut and choose to stagnate.

Let the Holy Spirit flow through your life in new and powerful ways. And tell everyone you know about Jesus; after all, that's why He baptized you in the Holy Spirit!

Want More?

For Reflection:

1. Have you ever felt spiritual stagnancy? What can you now do about it?

2. How can we make ourselves more sensitive to divine opportunities to minister to unbelievers?

10

For Those Who are Struggling to Receive

I began this book by relating my frustration and disappointment during years of not receiving the Spirit baptism.

I know what you are going through because I was a chronic seeker who just couldn't seem to receive. But I didn't quit trying and neither should you!

Don't make the mistake of thinking that God doesn't want to baptize you in His Spirit. God's Word is truer than our experiences.

Here are a few thoughts to help you encounter Jesus as your Baptizer in the Holy Spirit.

Why We Seek

Our basis for seeking is our hunger for more of God and more of His power to minister. However, the greater goal in seeking something from God is seeking God Himself.

Many are driven to receive the Spirit baptism or physical healing more than they are driven to know Christ. Because of our small human perspective we tend to put the least important needs in front of the greatest.

I have talked with people who have left a meeting after an extended time of seeking for the baptism in the Spirit and who were frustrated. They had prayed and worshipped for long hours and yet did not receive this gift. They began to wonder what was wrong with them. "Why can't I do it? What's standing in the way?" They were more concerned with apprehending the gift than gaining more of Jesus.

I have often shared that there is never a wasted moment in seeking Christ. Even when it appears that the answer you are looking for is never going to come, you have spent time with your best friend. Our heavenly Friend not only cares about us but also has the power to miraculously help us!

You haven't been "unsuccessfully seeking the baptism;" you have been "successfully seeking Jesus". That's time well spent!

Get Ready; Your Time Is Coming Soon!

If you are made of flesh, then it is

Want More?

God's will to baptize you in His Holy Spirit (see Acts 2:17).

Sometime soon, as you are pursuing Jesus, the Holy Spirit will come upon you. You then must dare to speak out, trusting Him to give you the new words. He will do it.

I once prayed with a gentleman to receive the baptism who was going nowhere in his seeking. I stopped and asked him how long he had sought. He replied, "Over fifty years!"

I then prayed, asking God to grant some insight into this man's long overdue baptism. The Lord showed me that He had given this gentleman some "funny sounding" words to speak the first time he ever prayed to receive. He also showed me that these same words were there every time this man sought the baptism, but the man would reject them.

I shared this insight with the man, and he began to weep. He told me that it was true, but he had always thought those funny-sounding words were just his imagination. He was afraid that he would somehow grieve or blaspheme the Holy Spirit when he spoke those words if they were from his imagination. But now he realized that they were from God.

I asked him what the words were. As he opened his mouth to say them, he began to speak in unlearned tongues fluently! He was suddenly baptized in the Holy Spirit!

Want More?

Those funny words were the first words of his new spiritual vocabulary. He had finally chosen to actively yield his speech to the Holy Spirit.

If you sense any sort of strange words, don't be afraid to speak them out. You will not grieve the Holy Spirit — you'll welcome Him. If you are seeking Jesus, it's safe!

Prayer

Father in heaven, I humbly ask You to baptize my friend in Your Holy Spirit right now. I welcome You, Jesus, to reveal Yourself as his/her Baptizer in the Holy Spirit. Please give my friend the faith and courage to speak Your new words now. Energize him/her to be an unstoppable soul-winner for You. In the mighty name of Jesus, Amen!

Want More?

About the Author

Tim Enloe and his wife, Rochelle, minister the Word and power of God through Spirit-anointed music, teaching, and personal altar ministry.

At their Conferences on the Holy Spirit, local churches and communities experience firsthand the Spirit's baptizing, healing, and transforming power.

The Enloes come from Godly families and endeavor to continue this heritage with their three sons: Braedon, Dolan, and Barret.

If you have received the Spirit baptism while reading this book or would like more information about their ministry, "Conference on the Holy Spirit," please contact:

Enloe Ministries /
Conference on the Holy Spirit
Post Office Box 780900
Wichita, Kansas 67278-0900
www.enloeministries.org

Additional Resources

Books, audio teaching series, worship music and other resources to help you grow and minister are available on our ministry website:

www.enloeministries.org